Heaven:
Can I Go?

JOYCE YATES

WESTBOW
PRESS
A DIVISION OF THOMAS NELSON

Scripture verses marked KJV are taken from the King James Version of the Bible.

Scripture verses marked NIV are taken from the Holy Bible, New International Version®. NIV®. Copyright ©1973, 1978, 1984 by International Bible Society. Used by permission of Zondervan. All rights reserved.

Scripture quotations notated The Message are taken from The Message: The Bible in Contemporary Language. Copyright ©1993, 1994, 1995, 1996, 2000, 2001, 2002. Used by permission of NavPress Publishing Group.

"Goin' Home," by Antonin Dvorak and William Arms Fisher, 1893. Reprinted with permission of Carl Fischer, LLC o/b/o Theodore Presser Company..

WestBow Press books may be ordered through booksellers or by contacting:

WestBow Press
A Division of Thomas Nelson
1663 Liberty Drive
Bloomington, IN 47403
www.westbowpress.com
1 (866) 928-1240

Because of the dynamic nature of the Internet, any web addresses or links contained in this book may have changed since publication and may no longer be valid. The views expressed in this work are solely those of the author and do not necessarily reflect the views of the publisher, and the publisher hereby disclaims any responsibility for them.

Any people depicted in stock imagery provided by Thinkstock are models, and such images are being used for illustrative purposes only. Certain stock imagery © Thinkstock.

ISBN: 978-1-4908-1242-7 (sc)
ISBN: 978-1-4908-1241-0 (e)

Library of Congress Control Number: 2013918583

Printed in the United States of America.

WestBow Press rev. date: 10/31/2013

To Marie (Mimi) Yates, my mother-in-law, who has served God and people for as long as I have known her. She truly is a living embodiment of abiding in Christ. Mimi's reservation has been made for many years, and she looks forward to that final trip in full confidence of meeting her loving Lord. Presently, ninety-four years of faith and love surround her daily.

Contents

Preface

I believe people in today's world are not concerned about eternity. Our last breath may come today, tomorrow, or sometime in the more distant future. We don't know when it will come, and that is why we need to prepare.

Christianity has taken a backseat to power, influence, wealth, and self-absorption. I hope this book will offer an alternative to all that; this was my faith-filled intention for writing it. The Lord has placed a desire in my heart to write a book that highlights eternity and His love and forgiveness. I believe He wants this book to comfort Christians and pose questions or plant seeds for non-Christians. As I age, my entire quest is to live a life that answers the call of the Holy Spirit in glorifying God through my actions on earth. The Lord has placed this book on my heart, and I have written the manuscript through His guidance. I really don't know the plan He has for it—whether it is to be a best seller, a book I give away when I speak at Christian functions, or simply a legacy for my children when I pass on to eternity. I do know for sure that the Lord led me to write it, and I have answered His call.

I beckon you to travel with me to a far country, a place where we will stay forever and ever. The preparation for the trip may take one or two years, or it may take eighty or ninety. The most important aspect of the trip is to have a solid reservation. I've already made mine; I invite you to make yours today.

Acknowledgments

This book would not have been possible without the skill and editing of my friend and former graduate assistant, Nicole Cobb. She possesses the talent to construct all of my notes, quotes, segments of pages, and writings into a beautiful finished product. I am truly grateful to Nicole for her daily demonstration of the fruit of the Spirit and for her unending kindness and love.

To my friend Kelly Powell, who graciously committed her skill as an artist by providing a drawing at the beginning of each chapter. Kelly dedicated each completed drawing to God's glory.

To my husband, Bill Yates, who stays positive in the midst of second-guessing myself and the value of my writing. He reminds me to remember it is all for the Lord's glory and honor.

And, to the unknown traveler who believes that once life is over, that is it. *Poof!* Just like that, you are gone. No more life, no heaven or hell—after death there is nothing. Because of you, I felt the need to write this book, which may pose a curiosity about heaven, my eternal home.

Introduction

❦

*I*f you are looking for a book that will lecture you into being a Christian, or one that will scold you into being a better man or woman of faith, you have opened the wrong book. This is not the intention. This book will support a keen look at the Savior's heavenly place of residence, and it will invite you to experience life on earth with a sense of joy and peace that surpasses human understanding. Open your mind and heart to explore this venture into an appreciation for a real eternal home. Develop delight, not dread, in anticipation of forever and ever.

If you are not a Christian, I invite you to navigate your way through this book as a tourist on a trip. Your passport for travel is a new understanding of what heaven is and how to claim it as your eternal home.

But remember, the first step is making your reservation. Let's be on our way . . .

> But as it is written, eye hath not seen, nor ear heard, neither have entered into the heart of man, the things which God hath prepared for them that love him.
> —1 Corinthians 2:9 (KJV)

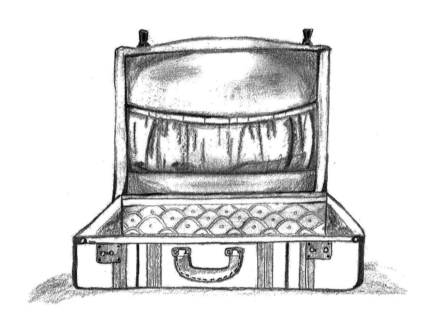

᪶ 1 ᪶

Ready for Your Trip?

*I*t was a warm day in Dallas, Texas. People gathered on the street in anticipation of seeing the thirty-fifth president of the United States. The motorcade was making its way past many excited onlookers. Jack Kennedy, better known as JFK, didn't wake up this November 22, 1963 morning thinking he was going to be assassinated. In fact, he, his wife, the Texas governor, and the governor's wife were riding in a convertible from Love Field to the Trade Mart, a ten-minute route for a slow motorcade. Five minutes away from the destination, gunshots were fired, and the president was dead.[1]

On August 30, 1997, Diana, Princess of Wales, arrived in Paris. After enjoying dinner and a late night out, a decoy automobile left the hotel, hoping to avert photographers. At the rear entrance of the hotel, Princess Di and her companion got into another vehicle, completely unaware of what was about to unfold. At half past midnight on August 31, the car crashed into a pillar in a tunnel in Paris. As a result of the internal injuries she sustained, Princess Di

---

[1] "November 22, 1963: Death of the President," John F. Kennedy Presidential Library and Museum, n.d., last accessed August 6, 2013, http://www.jfklibrary. org/JFK/JFK-in-History/November-22-1963-Death-of-the-President.aspx.

took her last breath at four o'clock that same morning. The world was stunned.[2]

Los Angeles was the perfect place for Michael Jackson to return in concert after many years of absence. He arrived at the Staples Center on June 24, 2009, for another rehearsal, one like so many others. The practice extended past midnight. The next afternoon, he had not come out of his bedroom. Found lying on his bed, with a weak pulse, he was rushed to the hospital, during which time the paramedics stated his condition as "full cardiac arrest." On June 25, 2009, at precisely 2:26 p.m., Michael Jackson was pronounced dead.[3]

I wonder if any of them had made their reservations. They each knew they would be going on a final trip . . . eventually. We all will. Many days preceded each of their final moments, but did that matter after those final breaths? Death levels the playing field. Power, prestige, money, fame, talent, and royalty all are gone at that point; none of it matters any longer. What does matter is whether each person has made that reservation for entrance into heaven. What about your reservation?

Multiple sources support that 1.8 people die every second in our world today. When will it be your turn? Life is a trip, all right. It has a pace that can be tough. Preparation for the end makes the present more appealing and livable. It is your choice whether or not you prepare. Plans for the last trip of your life must be intentional. What could be more important?

There is no guarantee of the next breath taken. There is no amount of money, talents, clout, possessions, personality traits, or fame that can grant anyone one more second on this earth. This life is a temporary residence, a vapor. Many people think that it

---

[2] "Princess Diana Dead after Paris Car Crash," Cable News Network, Inc., August 31, 1997, last accessed August 6, 2013, http://www.cnn.com/WORLD/9708/30/diana.dead/.

[3] "Michael Jackson," *The New York Times*, November 29, 2011, last accessed August 8, 2013, http://topics.nytimes.com/top/reference/timestopics/people/j/michael_jackson/index.html.

is all about chance—that is, you live a healthy, long life if you are lucky, and if you die young, you are just unlucky. However, is there really more to life's timetable than this? Is there more to the soul than just this life? Is heaven really a place? Is this life merely a temporary residence?

> Whereas ye know not what shall be on the morrow. For
> what is your life? It is even a vapour, that appeareth for
> a little time, and then vanisheth away.
> —James 4:14 (KJV)

> The grass withers and the flowers fall,
> because the breath of the Lord blows on them.
> Surely the people are grass.
> The grass withers and the flowers fall,
> but the word of our God stands forever.
> —Isaiah 40:7-8 (NIV)

The older you become, the more you realize the brevity of life and how important this trip is. Definitely the experiences and relationships of this life become more distinct with each advancing year. As you age, you attend the funerals of loved ones, friends, and acquaintances, and you wonder why you were spared the accident, disease, or unfortunate circumstance that ended in physical death for that person. Witnessing the deaths of loved ones, family members, and close friends may cause you to make plans in your own life, such as preparing your will and getting your life in order for when your time comes. Asking forgiveness for wrongdoings against others may also be on your agenda of preparation, and there is no sweeter peace than reconciliation. There is a reason for why you are alive today, and there is a greater purpose for you than what you can comprehend. Every day is a gift of 24 hours, or 1,440 minutes, or 86,400 seconds. Are you making the time count?

Count for what? That's a fair question for you to ask, but there is no simple answer. The answer lies in what you do to make every day on earth count for attaining entrance into your eternal home, for reaching your final destination. Would you look at life differently if you were told you had three days to live? Of course you would! You would immediately start making plans to visit close friends and family while you still had time. Living each and every day with a reservation for the final destination reminds you to proceed with valuable plans. These trip plans involve preparing daily for the awesome ultimate destination.

Exactly how does an eternal home fit into the picture of living every day as your last? Think about this. Do you enjoy leisure time and rest? Is your home a place you enjoy leaving for short trips or for visits with friends and family? Is this same home the place you long for if you are away for any length of time? Is your affection for home because it is a familiar place that harbors friends, family, and memories, and, most of all, love? Many people are wandering, searching for this type of home on earth, one where peace and love abound. Remember, a home on this earth may be overtaken by foreclosure, fire, relocation, calamity, or sadness; it is finite.

What about a home that is everlasting? Where is that home that abounds with peace, love, joy, comfort, family, friends, and complete goodness? Okay, now *that* sounds like a good deal, and it is. Start your plans, pack your bag, and make your reservation. Enjoy the preparation. It is full of adventure and great value! And, believe it or not, if everyone could read the trip reviews, they would want to go. Heaven is a home that is forever and ever! Interested?

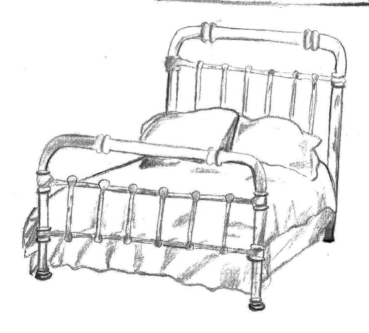

ᚖ 2 ᚖ

Sweet Sleep and Peace

$\mathcal{A}$ good night's sleep is important before you grab your ticket and go. Do you know how it feels to have a peaceful night's sleep? Your head hits the pillow, and you automatically fall asleep. The next morning, you awake fully rested, feeling peaceful and ready for your trip.

You may say that you are not going on your last trip today. Well, how do you know? You don't *know*, but you think you will definitely be alive for the next twenty-four hours. Hmm . . . who told you that? Perhaps the doctor told you your health was good and all your test results were excellent. Did he mention the driver you may meet on the road today? In 2011, 3,331 people were killed in crashes involving a distracted driver, and 387,000 people were injured in accidents involving a distracted driver, according to the National Highway Traffic Safety Administration.[4] Nearly thirty people die every day from drunk driving—that's one death every thirty-eight minutes, according to the United States Drunk

---

[4] National Highway Traffic Safety Administration, last accessed September 10, 2013, http://www.distraction.gov/content/get-the-facts/facts-and-statistics. html.

Driving Statistics.[5] Do you still think you are invincible? You never know when or how your time will come.

That brings us back to sleep and peace. You want a good trip planned and a reservation you can count on. You need to be well rested to accomplish this. Natural sleep is important for a good trip. A reservation gives you security and peace. I'll ask again, how many times have you experienced this type of sweet peace and sleep? Is it your normal nightly routine? Or has it become a thing of the past, something you never experience anymore—and if so, why?

Home should be a place of rest, a place where you can unwind and be content. Is your mind always racing about where you should be next, what piece of work did not get done, what action you haven't taken yet, or what relationship is breaking? Take a deep breath in, breathe out slowly, and relax. Peace is what home is all about—or what home *should* be all about. Let this thought go through your mind: live each day with your destination assurance— that is, eternal security. When you live in that way, your attitude, thoughts, values, and demeanor totally change. Most assuredly, your destination can be a peaceful, restful, and loving place.

Have you ever thought about heaven being the ultimate reservation, the best destination? "Okay," you say, "well, let me search Trip Advisor to see what they say about this destination." Careful—this isn't your normal trip advisor. This trip advisor is spelled B-I-B-L-E. Spend time searching it for the best deal or "most value"! You will not be disappointed.

Scripture offers us constant reminders of the ways to experience peace on earth, giving us a glimpse of what this final destination will be like.

> Come unto me, all ye that labour and are heavy laden,
> and I will give you rest. Take my yoke upon you, and
> learn of me; for I am meek and lowly in heart: and ye

---

5   United States Drunk Driving Statistics, last accessed September 10, 2013.
    http://visual.ly/united-states-drunk-driving-statistics.

shall find rest unto your souls. For my yoke is easy, and
my burden is light.

—Matthew 11:28-30 (KJV)

And we know that all things work together for good
to them that love God, to them who are the called
according to his purpose.

—Romans 8:28 (KJV)

In my Father's house are many rooms; if it were not
so, I would have told you. I am going there to prepare
a place for you.

—John 14:2 (NIV)

Do you toss and turn in bed, with your mind racing about
yesterday's mistakes, today's stress, or tomorrow's schedule? This
is *not* sweet peace and rest. Society screams, "If you can't sleep,
or if you worry too much, take a pill or have a drink." These two
options may hinder an easy journey to your ultimate destination.
Substance abuse will not give meaning to life. Don't substitute
worldly alternatives for spiritual peace. God assures us that His
yoke is easy and His burden is light, as mentioned above (Matthew
11:30 [KJV]).

Other words of Scripture also offer comfort in the middle of
the night, soothing the uneasiness of a racing mind:

Be still, and know that I am God.

—Psalm 46:10 (NIV)

Is this soothing comfort magic? No, it isn't magic, but it is a
miracle, and it is majestically relieving. God *wants* a relationship
with His children. During the middle of a sleepless night is the
perfect time to commune with Him. Place your burden at the foot
of the cross. Give it to *Him!* And then, trust Him. Envision heaven,
the final destination prepared for those who know Christ.

> Jesus said to her, I am the resurrection and the life. He who
> believes in me will live, even though he dies; and whoever
> lives and believes in me will never die. Do you believe this?
> —John 11:25-26 (NIV)

Love is comfort. Over and over again, the Bible tells us of God's unfailing unconditional love. God wraps His arms around us when we don't deserve it and haven't earned it, and simply through His grace and mercy, He supplies exactly what we need. Picture a father's unconditional love for his child. How much more does God our Father love us?

> If ye then, being evil, know how to give good gifts unto
> your children, how much more shall your Father which
> is in heaven give good things to them that ask him?
> —Matthew 7:11 (KJV)

With God, all you have to do is ask!

What does this world offer? Materialism, pain, sin, restlessness, sadness, and deceit. What does God offer? True peace, joy, forgiveness, rest, and truth. If you want the best life on this earth, seek the fruit of the Spirit, and watch the practice of these fruits transform the way you live.

> But the fruit of the Spirit is love, joy, peace, patience,
> kindness, goodness, faithfulness, gentleness and self-
> control. Against such things there is no law.
> —Galatians 5:22-23 (NIV)

Your earthly life becomes abundant in Christ, which is the closest thing to heaven on earth that anyone can attain.

A plan is extremely essential for a good trip to your destination. When preparing for a road trip, you will make sure that your car tank is full of gas, your bags are packed with appropriate clothing, and a first-aid kit is in the glove compartment. You've included some snacks in a bag, maps or GPS instruments for direction, and pillows for weary, tired passengers. If traveling by ship or plane, you prepare by having all identification documents for travel handy, and an itinerary of your temporary endeavor. This prepares you for peaceful, happy travel. In the same way, practicing and possessing the fruit of the Spirit allows you to go through this earthly life ready to travel, fully prepared and equipped with essential tools for endurance. "But the fruit of the Spirit is love, joy, peace, patience, kindness, goodness, faithfulness, [23] gentleness and self-control" (Galatians 5:22-23 [NIV]). Maturing in the fruit of the Spirit accompanies a life that has made a reservation for a heavenly home. This maturing is not automatic; rather, it comes with intentional plans, fully prepared as well as possible for the earthly life—this trip. Who would travel in cars, or on planes or ships, without bags or essential travel items? A similar principle applies to living a spirit-filled life on this earth while preparing for the reservation of a heavenly home. By possessing the fruit of the Spirit, life becomes more joyous through practicing these traits, which helps you see through God's perspective instead of the world's.

Sweet peace and good sleep can indicate a life dedicated to God's purposes, because *trust* is the true issue.

> Trust in the Lord with all thine heart; and lean not unto thine own understanding. In all thy ways acknowledge him, and he shall direct thy paths.
> —Proverbs 3:5-6 (KJV)

Trust—it's hard to muster in this visible, dog-eat-dog, fast-paced world, isn't it? Not really; it is simply a matter of how deliberate you are about your desire for truth and peace along your journey. Is your desire for sweet peace invested in a life that trusts and obeys, or one that is flippant about faith and inconsistent about dedication? Where are your mind and heart? If you have the largest home, the most expensive car, the latest technology, and the perfect physical body, but you can't sleep, you experience constant anxiety, and you are never satisfied, what have you accomplished? You won't ever find peace or rest in physical things. You find peace and rest solely in Christ. Ask Him, "Father, take over my mind, my thoughts, and protect me from straying from the peace offered by total trust in You."

Peace is intangible, yet it is more valuable than any material possession, and it is a by-product of intentional, faith-filled living. Embracing each day with heaven in mind during every step of your trip will promote intentional living for the Savior, the God of our earthly *and* eternal life. What have you got to lose? You don't want to lose your eternal home! If the Lord wakes you, study His Word. Find rest in Him.

> For we which have believed do enter into rest, as he said, As I have sworn in my wrath, if they shall enter into my rest: although the works were finished from the foundation of the world.
>
> —Hebrews 4:3 (KJV)

⌛ 3 ⌛

Why the World Does Not Want You to Take This Trip

🍂

$\mathcal{T}$ he world is full of sin and corruption. However, you do not have to choose to live as the rest of the world lives; instead, you can choose to carefully plan your trip by making a secure reservation. Yes, we are constantly surrounded by sin, but sin is not the only path. Your trip, both the path and the journey, can be filled with faith instead of sin.

Let's start with your luggage—fill it with the fruit of the Spirit to help guide you along the way. It is essential to pack your bag with these items, and it is equally essential to be intentional in your desire; in other words, carefully choose what to pack and what to leave behind. Ask simple, practical questions about what you do and don't want to take with you. It's much like the process of preparing for a regular trip: Pack this, not that; this wears well and doesn't wrinkle; this can go through a couple of wearings without washing. For the trip to the final destination, once recognizing what is and isn't essential, the process is much simpler and it only requires a small carry-on. Pack your bag with spiritual living, guided by Bible reading, meditation, and prayer.

Thy word is a lamp unto my feet, and a light unto my path.

—Psalm 119:105 (KJV)

The Lord's Word is a true path for life. It is not a guarantee that your circumstances will be without pain or misfortune, but a Christ-centered life is one that provides comfort and mercy during these times. It is also filled with purpose and meaning, making life less of a trip and more of a journey, with the ultimate destination of heaven always in sight.

Have I not commanded you? Be strong and courageous. Do not be afraid; do not be discouraged, for the Lord your God will be with you wherever you go.

—Joshua 1:9 (NIV)

The Lord has given humans the ability to make choices in this life. Whether those choices are wise or unwise is up to each individual person. With choices comes a responsibility, part of which involves remembering the sacrifices of our Savior. All this is part of packing for the trip and making the reservation.

Jesus died on the cross as a sacrifice for human sin. He died on the cross for whoever believes on Him, as mentioned in John 3:16. He is the ultimate sacrifice. Because of the death of Christ and His resurrection, we know that death is not the end.

And God shall wipe away all tears from their eyes; and there shall be no more death, neither sorrow, nor crying, neither shall there be any more pain: for the former things are passed away. And he that sat upon the throne said, Behold, I make all things new. And he said unto me, Write: for these words are true and faithful.

—Revelation 21:4-5 (KJV)

To prepare fully for the final destination and the ultimate reservation, we can be forgiven of our sin on this earth and seek to lead a life according to the will of God. The earth is not our eternal home; our eternal home is heaven but only for those who have believed in Christ, confessed all sins, and asked for forgiveness. This is the reservation, a free ticket full of God's mercy and grace. Oh, it is not deserved; you can't work for it. It is the winning ticket, paid in full and handed to you openly—a gift of true unconditional love, which Christians call "grace." This is the love and mercy freely given to us by God, as He desires for us to have it. We cannot do anything to earn it; we can only be willing to accept it from Him, and then we are free to reap the benefits. What a precious, truly invaluable gift!

The reservation is essential, but, remember, so are the contents of the travel bags. You had better start packing! A life guided by Bible reading and meditation must surely go in the bag; that cannot be overstated. Travel light, with simple essentials, and leave out all selfish and fleshly desires. "Light" in this sense means free and joyful, not empty. Placing confidence in circumstances, material possessions, and people is what will leave your bag empty. Material possessions can take up a lot of space in your bag; however, using them for God's glory and keeping these possessions low on the list of priorities is the key. How many times have circumstances, material possessions, and people been able to stop disease, provide comfort when accidents happen, or give peace to someone in perilous situations? The world shouts that "things" will satisfy you, that they will fill your empty life. But this is not true. Only hope, faith, and love will satisfy and fill you, and these come through belief in God the Father, the Son, and the Holy Spirit. Yes, we can derive satisfaction from relationships, but they have to be *real* relationships—first and foremost with Christ, and then with others. The world teaches giving in to fleshly desires. The Bible teaches faith and trust in Him, the perfect plan for life; so if you want a good trip, include it in your bag. Take the challenge to search the Bible for the best route to your final destination. The map for your trip has many options, and the safest, fastest, and most profitable one for you can be found in the Word of Truth. Steadfast, faithful trust in this is what will make heaven your final destination.

You need help, you say. You never pack alone! Need some advice? Go again to the ultimate trip advisor, your Bible. Turn to the Twenty-Third Psalm, and read the first line carefully:

> The Lord is my shepherd, I shall not be in want.
> —Psalm 23:1 (NIV)

Really take in what this means; take to heart the security of this plan. It doesn't mean that you never have any fleshly desires at all; but, rather, that your main desire is Christ, and that all other wants are secondary. There is a widely quoted saying of unknown origin that applies here as well: "Contentment is not the fulfillment of what you want; it is the realization of how much you already have." Live the abundant life in Christ. It is not an easy task; however, it is doable if the focus is on the destination—that is, heaven.

The world wants you to resist righteous living, to seek worldly success at all costs, and to do whatever you want to do. What have you gained if you have all the possessions you want but no one to share them with, no one who loves you for who you are and not what you own? What have you gained if your bank account is full, but your heart monitor has just flatlined? Are your hope and security in your possessions, or are they in your relationship with Christ? Possessions are temporary. Your relationship with Christ is eternal; your home in heaven is eternal.

With each chapter, you can see how increasingly valuable your reservation is. Your luggage is almost full, but with faith and the Spirit, not material things. Is the desire to make this reservation getting stronger? It will as you read on.

Ponder the parable of the farmer who filled all his warehouses with grain, hoarding the supply so that he would have plenty for a long time. This is a perfect illustration of earthly perception. Little did that farmer know that death was waiting for him that very night:

> Then he said to them, "Watch out! Be on your guard against all kinds of greed; a man's life does not consist in the abundance of his possessions." And he told them this parable: "The ground of a certain rich man produced a good crop. He thought to himself, 'What shall I do? I have no place to store my crops.' "Then he said, 'This is what I'll do. I will tear down my barns and build bigger ones, and there I will store all my grain and my goods. And I'll say to myself, "You have plenty of good things laid up for many years. Take life easy; eat, drink and be merry." "But God said to him, 'You fool! This very night your life will be demanded from you. Then who will get what you have prepared for yourself?' "This is how it will be with anyone who stores up things for himself but is not rich toward God."
> —Luke 12:15-21 (NIV)

What a different outcome that farmer would have enjoyed if he had made his reservation, packed his bag with the fruit of the Spirit and with Scripture, and spent time accepting the free ticket of mercy, grace, love, and peace. Instead, he spent all his time, effort, and energy on acquiring more, more, and more! He had to make sure that he had enough, and then more than enough, and, finally, more than he could possibly need. Oh, his bags were full all right: with earthly goods that decay with time. Why didn't he think about his eternal home, the life that is forever and ever? If he had, he would have realized that he already had enough and that he always would. There is always enough through God, through His perfect bounty, mercy, grace, and love—the abundance of heaven.

Do not store up for yourselves treasures on earth, where
moth and rust destroy, and where thieves break in and
steal. But store up for yourselves treasures in heaven,
where moth and rust do not destroy, and where thieves
do not break in and steal. For where your treasure is,
there your heart will be also.

—Matthew 6:19-21 (NIV)

Be careful for nothing; but in everything by prayer and
supplication with thanksgiving let your requests be
made known unto God.

—Philippians 4:6 (KJV)

↜ 4 ↝

The Road Map

So far, you understand about your trip, your luggage, your reservation, and your ultimate destination. What about the journey? Your journey on earth is the road map, which includes the study of God's Word.

In his book *The Case for Christ*, Lee Strobel reveals a historical investigation of the truth of the words of the Bible. Formerly an atheist, Strobel worked as an investigative reporter for the *Chicago Tribune*. Strobel cross-examined experts to question the truth of the Scriptures and biblical Christianity. Any skeptic of the truth of God's Word should read Strobel's book. To briefly summarize his conclusions, the authenticity of the Scripture in the Holy Bible is absolutely genuine; every word is God-breathed and placed on each page of the Bible by God-appointed apostles. When examining the history of biblical times and the events recounted in the Bible, Strobel found that the truths conveyed are consistent with historical research and, therefore, accurate. The bottom line to Strobel's discovery is that God is the Father, Son, and Holy Spirit who provides purpose, not only in this life, but for all eternity. God provides a love that can only be understood by those who accept His mercy and grace. The Bible is ultimate Truth.[6]

The conclusions of Strobel, the former atheist, have been in Scripture all along, cherished and embraced by believers throughout the ages. Understand that before Christ became the covenant sacrifice for all sin, the Old Testament covenants for God's people directed rules for living. Problems occurred with obeying these covenants because no human living in a fallen world could abide by all the rules. It was impossible. After Jesus' sacrificial death on the cross, the new covenant of Jesus Christ as the heavenly high priest took reign. Jesus, the ultimate sacrifice, died for all sins. No longer were the rules of the Old Testament covenants needed to guide externally, as Christ became the new covenant for believers, living internally in the hearts of believers as the Holy Spirit. What a gift! The history and creation of the Old Testament covenants are still important to remember; however, God's gift of mercy and grace through His Son, Jesus Christ, allows believers to live unconditionally in love and forgiveness. No animal sacrifice is necessary. Jesus was and is the ultimate sacrifice for sin. The Old Testament covenants, particularly the Ten Commandments, provide insight into blessing still today; however, they do so with a new enabling guide, the Holy Spirit.

> This is the covenant I will establish with the people of Israel after that time, declares the Lord. I will put my laws in their minds and write them on their hearts. I will be their God, and they will be my people. No longer will they teach their neighbor, or say to one another, 'Know the Lord,' because they will all know me, from the least of them to the greatest. For I will forgive their wickedness and will remember their sins no more.
> —Hebrews 8:10-12 (NIV)

---

[6] Lee Strobel, *The Case for Christ* (Grand Rapids, Mich.: Zondervan, 1998).

God instructed Moses to impress upon the Israelites the importance of keeping all of His decrees and commands for a life of blessing:

> And these words, which I command thee this day, shall be in thine heart: And thou shalt teach them diligently unto thy children, and shalt talk of them when thou sittest in thine house, and when thou walkest by the way, and when thou liest down, and when thou risest up. And thou shalt bind them for a sign upon thine hand, and they shall be as frontlets between thine eyes. And thou shalt write them upon the posts of thy house, and on thy gates.
>
> —Deuteronomy 6:6-9 (KJV)

> If the Lord delights in a man's way, he makes his steps firm.
>
> —Psalm 37:23 (NIV)

> Trust in the Lord with all your heart
> and lean not on your own understanding;
> in all your ways acknowledge him,
> and he will make your paths straight.
>
> —Proverbs 3:5-6 (NIV)

> Call to me and I will answer you and tell you great and unsearchable things you do not know.
>
> —Jeremiah 33:3 (NIV)

Family and friends need to understand the importance of your road map. Make wise decisions according to biblical direction. Talk about this at your dinner table, display it in your actions, and model the life filled with the safekeeping of the final destination. Security about love and eternal life is in the name of God. A Christian who exercises confidence in faith is a role model for those around them. Family and friends view how a Christian reacts to stressful situations and traumatic events. Coworkers and colleagues marvel at the way of life of a Christian, who always displays an attitude of gratefulness for the blessings of everyday moments.

Do you react to your good and bad times with a faith that is unfaltering? Does your road map influence your decisions, statements, and attitude?

Life does not end when the physical body dies. Christians strive for unfaltering faith while looking forward to the rest of the story in eternity. This is security in that final reservation for the ultimate destination. True Christians always live with heaven in mind, each and every day of their life on earth.

I do not want to go, but if I do go, I am ready! Think about this. Would you be ready to go if you were suddenly faced with death? You may not want to leave this life, but the moment that you do leave isn't up to you. Will you be ready when that moment comes? Are you ready now? Remember, that moment may come at any time, in any place, and in any form. There is only one way to be ready.

People spend time securing life insurance policies, building big bank accounts, and acquiring the biggest, best, and newest possessions. Is this the legacy you prefer? What about cultivating steadfast and loving relationships, service beyond comprehension, peace not fathomable, and the assurance of your final destination? Remember that your ticket is free. The road map is available. The choice is yours. That reservation is sounding better and better, and the journey to your ultimate destination is beginning to be the best trip ever!

Use the road map for direction. God has given His Word through the Bible to teach us how to live well and how to have abundant life. This does not mean life without suffering. It means a life that is dependent upon Him. When we suffer, God gives us the strength to endure that suffering, to survive, and to emerge stronger and wiser. He is also there during good, great, and happy times. No matter the circumstances, rest in the security and peace of knowing a Father in heaven who loves and provides an eternal home just for you.

There is no better compass to have for your trip than the Ten Commandments. These commands help keep you on the right path, guiding you to reach your destination, and they are helpful when you encounter other people along the way.

> *Jesus gives us permanent forgiveness because His death was a one-time payment-in-full for all sins ever committed—even future ones. No mere human could obey every aspect of all of the divine commandments handed down through Moses. But Christ fulfilled the Law for us, and grace makes it count on our behalf. Our Savior sacrificed His life for us, and as a result, we can approach God's throne directly.*[7]

A Small Group Study series states that "Religion operates on the principle of 'I obey—therefore I am accepted by God.' The basic operating principle of the gospel is 'I am accepted by God through the work of Jesus Christ—therefore I obey.'"[8] It may be difficult to uphold these commandments that we have been given, yet striving daily to abide by these instructions is the most effective way to live as Christ does.

> God spoke all these words: I am God, your God, who brought you out of the land of Egypt, out of a life of slavery. No other gods, only me. No carved gods of any size, shape or form of anything whatever, whether of things that fly or walk or swim. Don't bow down to them and don't serve them because I am God, your God . . . No using the name of God, your God, in curses or silly

---

[7] Charles F. Stanley, "Daily Devotions: Living by Grace," *In Touch* (July 2013): 57.
[8] Timothy Keller, *The Prodigal God: Finding Your Place at the Table* (Grand Rapids, Mich.: Zondervan, 2011).

banter . . . Observe the Sabbath day, to keep it holy . . .
Honor your father and mother so that you'll live a long
time in the land that God, your God, is giving you. No
murder. No adultery. No stealing. No lies about your
neighbor. No lusting after your neighbor's house—or
wife or servant or maid or ox or donkey. Don't set your
heart on anything that is your neighbor's.

—Exodus 20:1-17 (*The Message*)[9]

Even though these Ten Commandments were given to Moses
for the Israelites in the Old Testament, the means of salvation
throughout history have always been God's mercy and grace.
Accepting God's gift of salvation and following His call for
abundant living and abiding in His will forever is His free gift
to you. When God so emphatically gives believers a blueprint for
living an abundant life, why would you need to read any other
books to learn how to succeed?

The Bible continues to be the best-selling book on the market
throughout the world. Though written in ancient times, it has
never lost its importance or relevance. Delving into Scripture and
praying for understanding will open avenues of commitment to
Christ and provide a road map that never changes. Christ becomes
the heart's desire, and heaven the long-awaited eternal home.

The Lord hath prepared his throne in the heavens; and
his kingdom ruleth over all.

—Psalm 103:19 (KJV)

And the God of all grace, who called you to his eternal
glory in Christ, after you have suffered a little while,
will himself restore you and make you strong, firm
and steadfast.

---

[9]   Eugene H. Peterson, *The Message: The Bible in Contemporary Language*
(Colorado Springs, Colo.: NavPress Publishing Group, 1993).

—1 Peter 5:10 (NIV)

These things I have spoken unto you, that in me ye
might have peace. In the world ye shall have tribulation:
but be of good cheer; I have overcome the world.
—John 16:33 (KJV)

Oh yes, God has overcome the world, and He walks with us
on earth today—even if we don't see Him, we still know that He
is there. How reassuring it is to know that God wants to be our
helper, living within us, guiding us in all areas of life. So live each
day with heaven in mind. If only we were more concerned with
eternity than with our current temporary home!

But the Counselor, the Holy Spirit, whom the Father
will send in my name, will teach you all things and will
remind you of everything I have said to you.
—John 14:26 (NIV)

5

The Last Trip Really Matters

Jane was about six years old when her mother and father went to say good-bye to a friend before he went to heaven. They took her with them into the house for the viewing of their deceased friend. Jane's parents told her to sit on the couch while they walked over to the casket, viewed the body, and expressed sympathy to the family. Afterward, Jane asked her parents many questions about death and heaven. She dreamed that she had seen the body in the casket. The conversations she overheard seemed strange to her, and she found the entire experience eerie. She had not thought about death until that day, and she continued to ask questions. Jane, at the tender age of six, didn't understand what the last trip was all about. Her parents gave her the best answers they could, but their answers depended on their own reservations. Jane wondered if her mother and father would go with her on this final trip. Although difficult and frightening for children to understand, as adults we must recognize that the last trip is an individual one, but many of us, regardless of age, are no more aware of the requirements than an average six-year-old. Jane wasn't sure how to plan for this trip, what she needed to pack, and how she could make her reservation. She really wasn't sure how to go. How many of us are sure of what to do and how to go? Are *you* sure of what to do and how to go?

Do you remember your first experience with death? Did you watch a family member die? Was your first experience with death attending the funeral of a family member or friend? When the trip up to that point has been uncertain, when there is no certainty that the reservation is secure, the entire process of death tends to leave us with questions that are hard to answer, filling us with despair and anxiety. It's easy to feel as scared as a six-year-old! Is this trip beginning to get a little too personal? Are you thinking about your reservation, wondering if you should make it now? Don't hesitate—make it *now*, today.

> In my Father's house are many mansions: if it were not so, I would have told you. I go to prepare a place for you. And if I go and prepare a place for you, I will come again, and receive you unto myself; that where I am, there ye may be also.
>
> —John 14:2-3 (KJV)

> So then after the Lord had spoken unto them, he was received up into heaven, and sat on the right hand of God.
>
> —Mark 16:19 (KJV)

> And Jesus said unto him, Verily I say unto thee, To day shalt thou be with me in paradise.
>
> —Luke 23:43 (KJV)

Paradise . . . really? That sounds like a great trip! I'll bet it costs a lot of money. You might think so, but the truth is that it doesn't cost a penny. In fact, it is a free gift, wrapped with love, forgiveness, mercy, and grace. The invitation to make your reservation, pack your bags, and begin this trip will transform you, helping you to realize that you are a sinner in need of a Savior. Once you acknowledge this, all you need to do is ask forgiveness for your sins, accept Christ as Savior, and thus receive the gift of salvation and eternal life.

> For all have sinned and fall short of the glory of God.
> —Romans 3:23 (NIV)

Remain mindful that the experience of accepting Jesus Christ as Savior and Lord with forgiveness of sins is a personal occurrence. Trust that your faith will grow as you maintain that personal relationship with Jesus through prayer, Bible reading, and meditation on His Word. Your life *will* be transformed. You may accept the Savior in a vast crowd of people, or you may receive salvation when you are alone, in the quiet of your own room. The crowd is not what matters—all that matters is your commitment to a new life in Christ. After receiving salvation, you will begin this journey of trusting in the quiet confidence and peace that the Holy Spirit provides for you.

How do you prepare for such an amazing journey, the one that ends when you arrive in the place called heaven? One of the best ways to prepare is by worshipping the Lord and praising Him in your everyday life, the journey. Giving glory and honor to Him who brought you into the world that He created is the best thing you can do, and it is what pleases Him most. Love God and also love other people. This provides a wonderful example for how He loves us and desires the best for us. Human language falls short of describing heaven's majesty. To understand such a wonderful place, you must have an open and focused mind when reading, meditating, and studying the Bible. Your understanding will then be imbued with God's wisdom and grace.

Prayer is a vital part of the Christian life, and it is essential to an intimate relationship with Christ. Prayer strengthens the Christian and allows comfort in times of distress. God calls us to abide in Him. Abiding is placing our trust in Him and growing in a faith that leads to the final reservation.

Ask and it will be given to you; seek and you will find; knock and the door will be opened to you. For everyone who asks receives; the one who seeks finds; and to the one who knocks, the door will be opened.
—Matthew 7:7-8 (NIV)

If ye abide in me, and my words abide in you, ye shall ask what ye will, and it shall be done unto you.
—John 15:7 (KJV)

God invites you to talk with Him. He wants to not only be your spiritual father but also your friend. Tell Him about your life, your struggles, your desires, and your faith. Prayer allows the opportunity to commune and to praise.

Delight yourself in the Lord, and he will give you the desires of your heart.
—Psalm 37:4 (NIV)

Pray often and fervently. Comfort, love, and peace will abound. Prayer will not always be answered in the manner we prefer; however, it always works out for our good and for His glory. Remember, prayer is not about the one praying, but about God's will. Through prayer, a believer is transformed into understanding God's will and His ways. The focus shifts from *me* to *Him*. Grow in your conversations with God. Prayer is necessary for a smooth ride on your trip. The journey is now; the eternal destiny is tomorrow. Become familiar with the reservation specialist in heaven by conversing with Him now.

If you love me, you will obey what I command. And I will ask the Father, and he will give you another Counselor to be with you forever—the Spirit of truth. The world cannot accept him, because it neither sees

him nor knows him. But you know him, for he lives with you and will be in you. I will not leave you as orphans; I will come to you. Before long, the world will not see me anymore, but you will see me. Because I live, you also will live. On that day you will realize that I am in my Father, and you are in me, and I am in you. Whoever has my commands and obeys them, he is the one who loves me. He who loves me will be loved by my Father, and I too will love him and show myself to him.
—John 14:15-21 (NIV)

Jesus answered, "I am the way and the truth and the life. No one comes to the Father except through me."
—John 14:6 (NIV)

If you have never believed in Christ, these biblical truths may be hard for you to understand. Simply put, God loves you more than any person or thing ever could. By having a relationship with Him through His Son, Jesus, you can have that promise of an eternity in heaven, and you can live a full and enriched life by trusting in His promises. When you study His Word, you learn more about the character of God and how His love and compassion are immeasurable and unceasing. Daily realize that in this world, we all are helpless sinners in need of God's grace and mercy. It is difficult to fully comprehend God's grace. Our sole purpose in this life is to glorify Him and to live in a way that will honor Him, and we do this by striving to follow His ways and by loving His people in the process.

The cross where Jesus died is a reminder that He died for *all* sins. What a wonderful discovery to make on a trip: cultivating a life lived with forgiveness and grace. To receive the Lord as Savior, a person must admit that he or she is a sinner, repent of his or her sins, believe and trust in Christ, and walk in faith.

For God so loved the world, that he gave his only
begotten Son, that whosoever believeth in him should
not perish, but have everlasting life.

—John 3:16 (KJV)

Confess your sins, and ask Jesus to be living and active in your
life. Accept forgiveness as a free gift of God's mercy and grace
by means of the ultimate sacrifice: Jesus' death on the cross for
all sin. At that very moment of acceptance, you have made your
reservation; your trip becomes a life of faith on this earth, and you
have the blood of Jesus as your luggage, packed with the fruit of
the Spirit.

Once you are saved and have eternal life in Christ, your
name is written in the Lamb's Book of Life, the log of heavenly
reservations. This book is a list of all those people—past, present,
and future—who accept Jesus Christ as their Lord and Savior. As
soon as you commit your life to Christ and begin your relationship
with Him, you are eternally His, and your security and hope can
never be lost. Your hope and security are in the Lord, and He will
never leave you or forsake you. You will live with Christ as your
personal Savior.

Be strong and of a good courage, fear not, nor be afraid
of them: for the Lord thy God, he it is that doth go with
thee; he will not fail thee, nor forsake thee.

—Deuteronomy 31:6 (KJV)

Salvation is found in no one else, for there is no other
name under heaven given to mankind by which we
must be saved.

—Acts 4:12 (NIV)

He who believes in Christ shall live forever—for to be absent
with the physical body is to be alive with the Lord! As believers,

we have a promise and a guarantee for a new life in Christ once our time on earth has finished.

> We always thank God, the Father of our Lord Jesus Christ, when we pray for you, because we have heard of your faith in Christ Jesus and of the love you have for all God's people—the faith and love that spring from the hope stored up for you in heaven and about which you have already heard in the true message of the gospel that has come to you. In the same way, the gospel is bearing fruit and growing throughout the whole world—just as it has been doing among you since the day you heard it and truly understood God's grace.
> —Colossians 1:3-6 (NIV)

> He hath made everything beautiful in his time: also he hath set the world in their heart, so that no man can find out the work that God maketh from the beginning to the end.
> —Ecclesiastes 3:11 (KJV)

Regardless of whether we individually pursue the burning desire to know God and to live eternally, doing so is a choice that He gives all people. In asking for forgiveness of sin and accepting Jesus Christ as the Son of God, we can proclaim Him as our Lord and Savior, and then we can know His peace. This peace, again, is rest in knowing that eternity is in our hearts and waiting for us no matter what day or time we are called. It doesn't matter when you go, you will be prepared.

> But godliness with contentment is great gain. For we brought nothing into this world, and it is certain we can carry nothing out.
> —1 Timothy 6:6-7 (KJV)

While we look not at the things which are seen, but at the things which are not seen: for the things which are seen are temporal: but the things which are not seen are eternal.

—2 Corinthians 4:18 (KJV)

Peace I leave with you, my peace I give unto you: not as the world giveth, give I unto you. Let not your heart be troubled, neither let it be afraid.

—John 14:27 (KJV)

If ye then be risen with Christ, seek those things which are above, where Christ sitteth on the right hand of God. Set your affection on things above, not on things on the earth.

—Colossians 3:1-2 (KJV)

Live each day with heaven in mind. Don't hesitate—make your reservation today. Pack your bags, grab your road map and compass, and get ready. Your Guide is with you and will never let you down. You will have the best trip you've ever had—it's absolutely guaranteed!

Notes

Keller, Timothy. *The Prodigal God: Finding Your Place at the Table*. Grand Rapids, Mich.: Zondervan, 2011.

Lewis, C. S. *Mere Christianity*. London: Fount, 1997.

"Michael Jackson." *The New York Times*. November 29, 2011. Last accessed August 8, 2013. http://topics.nytimes.com/top/reference/timestopics/people/j/michael_jackson/index.html.

National Highway Traffic Safety Administration. Last accessed September 10, 2013. http://www.distraction.gov/content/get-the-facts/facts-and-statistics.html.

"November 22, 1963: Death of the President." John F. Kennedy Presidential Library and Museum. n.d. Last accessed August 6, 2013. http://www.jfklibrary.org/JFK/JFK-in-History/November-22-1963-Death-of-the-President.aspx.

Peterson, Eugene H. *The Message: The Bible in Contemporary Language*. Colorado Springs, Colo.: NavPress Publishing Group, 1993.

"Princess Diana Dead after Paris Car Crash." Cable News Network, Inc. August 31, 1997. Last accessed August 6, 2013. http://www.cnn.com/WORLD/9708/30/diana.dead/.

Stanley, Charles F., "Daily Devotions: Living by Grace," *In Touch* (July 2013): 57.

Strobel, Lee. *The Case for Christ*. Grand Rapids, Mich.: Zondervan, 1998.

United States Drunk Driving Statistics. Last accessed September 10, 2013. http://visual.ly/united-states-drunk-driving-statistics.

"Going Home" by Antonin Dvorak
Lyrics by William Arms Fisher

Going home, Going home. I'm a going home.
Quiet-like, some still day, I'm just going home.
It's not far, just close by, Through an open door.
Work all done, care laid by, Going to fear no more.
Mother's there, expecting me, Father's waiting too.
Lots of folk gathered there, All the friends I know.

Nothing's lost, all's gain, No more fear or pain,
No more stumbling by the way, No more longing for the day,
Going to roam no more.

Morning star lights the way, Restless dreams all done.
Shadows gone, break of day, Real life has begun.
There's no break, there's no end, Just a living on.
Wide awake with a smile, going on and on . . .

Going home, going home, I'm just going home.
It's not far, just close by, Through an open door.
I am going home . . . I'm just going home.

43

For God so loved the world that he gave his only begotten Son, that whosoever believeth in him should not perish, but have everlasting life. – John 3:16 (KJV)

Now faith is being sure of what we hope for and certain of what we do not see. – Hebrews 11:1 (NIV)

About the Author

♥

Dr. Joyce Yates has served in her local church as a teacher for over thirty years. She believes in the value of faith, family, and friends. Having concern over the state of society and its enticement with earthly treasures, Dr. Yates has written this book to bring and renew the majesty of heaven back into the focus of individuals.

CPSIA information can be obtained at www.ICGtesting.com
Printed in the USA
LVOW05s1545061213

364192LV00001B/23/P